JOHNNY DEPP

BOOK

The Biography of
Johnny Depp

ALLEN GREGORY BURTON

Table of Content

Introduction

On June 9, 1963, Hollywood actor John Christopher Depp II was born in the U.S. Johnny Depp's dad was a civil engineer, and his mom was a waitress and a housewife. After the death of Depp's grandfather, he was moved to Florida, where he was raised with his sisters Debbie and Christi Dembrowski, who later became personal managers, and his older brother D.P. Depp, who is now a screenwriter. They all lived together there. Depp did drop out of Loft Studio school in Los Angeles, California, a year after his parents split up at the age of 16. Johnny Depp played guitar as a child, and he wanted to pursue his dream of becoming a musician by joining a band called "The Flame" with his friends in the early 1980s. The band toured the nightclubs in Florida but later became known as "The Kids" after they secured an opening gig for Iggy Pop, featuring Johnny Depp on lead vocals. He got his big break in acting through Fox Network's TV show, 21 Jump Street, from which he landed a starring role in Oliver Stone's Platoon, released in 1986. He survived the perils of adolescent heartthrob fame to become a respected adult actor. Depp has worked with Tim Burton many times, and he has done well in a number of critically acclaimed films. His eccentric personality has earned him recognition as a great performer, despite being called unconventional. This has surprised critics who thought he was just another photogenic Tiger Beat star.

Despite this huge success, or maybe because of it, Johnny Depp's career took a turn for the worse after a string of smash-hit failures. A lot of people were worried about Johnny Depp after movies like The Tourist, Dark Shadows, and The Lone Ranger didn't do well with audiences and critics. They made people wonder when Depp's career would get back on track. In 2016, he lent his voice as the Mad Hatter in Alice Through the Hall of

Mirrors and started work on the fourth
Pirates movie.

Chapter One

Birth and early childhood

In Owensboro, which may be a small town, but it's not just one of those sleepy country towns that we love to idealize in romantic comedies, because ultimately, as much as we like to pretend, small towns don't always have it all together. They have their fair share of issues, challenges, and problems too. But what they lack in size, they make up for with integrity and sincerity. So next time you're looking for a cute romance set back in the place you grew up, remember that a small town is the perfect setting for any type of realistic story because people are more relatable there than anywhere else in general. The city of Owensboro, Kentucky is one of the most exciting places in the country to call home, thanks in large part to its having its own charter and being a home rule class, which allows for more flexibility than other cities. It's also where John Christopher Depp II was born on June 9th, 1963. In addition to his mother, Betty Sue, he has a father, John Christopher Depp Sr. The mom works at a coffee shop. It's been reported that Johnny has always been close to and admired his mother, who raised him and his siblings with selflessness and affection. He refers to his mother, whom he calls "mum," as having worked diligently to cater to their needs when they were born and raised. As the smallest of four kids, he has always maintained a tight relationship with his siblings from a prior marriage. The brothers, Danny (also known as DP and screenwriter today), Debbie (also known as DP and screenwriter), and Christie (also known as Johnny's personal assistant), are all 10 years older than him.

Lightning bugs, creatures that are both interesting and lovely, are among Johnny's earliest childhood memories. Johnny insists that his family started to refer to him as "Johnny" early on in his childhood. Additionally, he is referred to by some of his siblings as "Dippity Dog" and "Johnny Dip", while others opt for "Dog Head". A close second in Johnny's life was his grandpa, whom he affectionately addressed as "Paw Paw." Johnny adored his grandfather. When he was a child, Johnny remembers harvesting tobacco with him in the fields and paying attention to his dad's tales. Johnny was devastated when his grandpa died since he had spoken about how close they were. When asked how he coped with his grandfather's death, Johnny admitted to dealing with it in a supernatural way, as he started to sense his grandfather's closeness to him. According to him, this behavior has "persisted throughout his life, particularly during moments of difficulty."

When he was seven years old, his family relocated to Miramar, Florida, where they lived in hotels for a long period until his dad was hired as the director-general of public works. "There were two grocery shops that confronted each other, and little really occurred there," explains Johnny, who grew up in Miramar. There were at least twenty homes they resided in by the time Johnny was a teenager. "It might awaken old memories of relocating," he says as he packs his bag to embark on one of his numerous journeys. After moving, Johnny's wild side came out as he felt a sense of insecurity and instability in his life. As for Johnny, he felt like a strange child who aspired to be Daniel

Boone to Bruce Lee as a youngster. As he matured, Johnny's attention shifted to music. As a result of his uncle's work as a pastor, his gospel choir often played at church services. Johnny noted how engaged the crowd was with what his uncle was saying as he stepped on stage and signaled for them to come around. After only a few sentences, it became evident that he was less concerned with the substance of his speech than he was with how music affected his listeners. Their music would not have been complete without the screams and roars of Eddie, Danny's brother, who really contributed to their sound by providing wailing solos and loud riffs. Through his rock-loving brother, Johnny was exposed to Van Morrison, Kiss, and Bob Dylan. To Johnny's dismay, he became crazier and more delusional. Recklessness and danger were two things he was enamored with. Evil Knievel was one of the roles he portrayed during World War II. Because he remained friendless and bullied at school, Johnny learned how to protect himself. He makes a request to build tunnels under the yard at school, and his teacher agrees. As a result of the bullying he endured in school and his own sense of alienation, Johnny developed into a daydreamer who got into a lot of trouble. His grades began to fall because of the harsh tutelage he received from one teacher who brooked no nonsense. His grades began to fall because of the reason he had been chosen as a scapegoat. Before he exited the room, Johnny mooed her and lowered his trousers.

As a result of his suspension, Johnny was demoted and branded a troublemaker. With his buddies, he started to do stunts like dousing a shirt in gasoline and setting it on fire in an attempt to mimic Gene Simmons' fire-eating feat. It backfired for a single second, and Johnny's face was scorched. When Johnny's mother arrived home that night, he pretended to be burnt by pyrotechnics so that he wouldn't get in trouble. He began to engage in ordinary pranks, such as egging automobiles, and school was put on hold.

In order to satisfy Johnny's obsession with the acoustic guitar, his mother purchased him one for $25 from one of his uncles' gospel groups. Johnny then spent almost a year locked up in his room practicing until he was proficient on the instrument. His love of music blossomed into a new calling, and he was able to express his deepest dreams through it. Flame was the name of his first band, which he began playing in small garage bands. Johnny was not only a talented musician, but he was also a master of the rock 'n' roll lifestyle's visual esotericism. He began stealing his mother's clothing and began to "wear her velour blouses and seasucker bellbottoms." One of his regrets in life is that he "simply couldn't locate any" pairs of platform shoes. Aside from Peter Frampton, Brahms, and Mozart, Johnny claims to have loved all kinds of music, including whatever he could get his hands on at the time. One of the little boy's favorite pastimes was watching and mimicking his older brother. Anything he would pick up, from playing his guitar to speaking a new language skillfully, Johnny found a way to copy it. However, Johnny's academics were not progressing smoothly. In his third year of high school, he claimed to only have around eight credits and to be completely disinterested in school. He was an outcast and a member of the negative gang. It didn't matter whether he brought his guitar to school; he'd always head to the rehearsal rooms to play. He is the first to acknowledge that his adolescent years were not full of good deeds after drinking, smoking, and bursting into school and damaging just about whatever he could, "he was only 12 years old. Among his newfound circle of musically inclined buddies, Johnny found his "place in life" as he pursued his aspirations of rock and roll success. He dropped out of school when he was just 16 years old and went to bars with his band members. He paid them off by carrying a fake ID that allowed him entry even though alcohol wasn't legal for children. Despite the fact that Johnny was still too young to legally drink, a lot of the older people present in these places took advantage of his age and status as one of the only minors around. The singer, named Johnny, had sex with an ex-girlfriend of one of his bandmates in her car behind a building near their school. The Flame bassist's blue Ford van was their first place to sleep together. Johnny claims that they were romantically involved for a brief period of time before losing contact. By the time he was fourteen, Johnny had "done just about every sort of drug there was," he claims. There was a feeling of approaching destruction in his eyes, as well as the acknowledgment that the wide range of various adolescents, in a similar way, were going nowhere. With development and a comprehension of the results of his activities, his choice to dial back was a shrewd one. His parents disclosed their separation when he was on the verge of this realization.

Despite the fact that the split was not a complete shock to everybody, Johnny reacted strongly and emotionally, saying he could recall his parents' arguing with the children in the next hallway, listening. Depp got down to business and assumed the errand of ameliorating his mom and keeping her peppy. He told her, with epic tendency, that he was more stressed over her fulfillment than he was about his own longing. Johnny has expressed that he felt a sense of urgency to assist his mom with adapting to the deficiency of her mom. With Johnny still on good terms, Lori recommended him to her friend Nicholas Cage because she believed he had a particular gift.

Nicholas had previously acted in Rumblefish, making him a well-known performer in his own right. Nicholas and Johnny got along like old buddies straight away. Nicholas urged Johnny to seek a profession as an entertainer. Aside from getting some much-needed cash, acting may help Johnny fund his music career. At first, Johnny scoffed at the idea. To meet the agent, Nicholas, Johnny went with him. Right away, she fell in love with Johnny, and she signed him up regardless of his lack of prior professional experience, much to his dismay. She instructed Johnny to go to an audition for a new Wes Craven picture as the first task he was given. Johnny was apprehensive when he viewed the script. Football jocks are often tall and blond. Johnny's outfit of choice for the audition was earrings and poofy hair. He turned up for the role looking like a fucking burial chamber inhabitant, "he said, laughing. Johnny, on the other hand, had already prepared for the audition and nailed the lines. He couldn't disguise his charisma or charm, and he had no trouble winning the director over. The daughter of Craven's killer was in the audience, and she and her pals were blown away by Johnny's seductive charms. After seeing this, Wes felt compelled to go all in and give Johnny the part. Johnny was overjoyed to get paid at all, despite his low expectations. Whether or not Johnny really took hamburgers from the seven-eleven to eat is unknown, but it is clear that he was desperate for cash at the time. A self-confessed "deadass broke" man, Even after six years in the music business, Johnny was not anticipating or prepared for instant success in the music industry. During his six-week stint on the set, he earned between $1,200 and $1,500 each week, a sum he had never seen before. He was stunned that people were always willing to pay him so much money. A sudden burst of inspiration prompted Johnny to take on this new challenge, reading up on acting skills and attempting to become more dedicated to the dramatic parts he really desired. Aside from The Nightmare on Elm Street, which was a huge hit, Johnny had a terrible time finding work after that. He accepted whatever position he could get to keep acting as his only source of income. His next appearance was in Laurie Frank's student film, "Dummies." A young actress called Sherilyn Fenn was hired as his co-star, and the two hit it off so well on set that they quickly began dating and eventually fell head over heels in love. They met when they were both twenty-two years old and immediately began living together. They dated for a time before deciding to marry. Johnny's band, The Kids, disbanded around this time, and he doesn't publicly discuss a black and white chronology for this period in his life. Sources have cited Johnny as stating, "yes... they still hate me," while other sources have described him as claiming he was too busy acting and performing in the band The Rock Angels at the time of their breakup.

On the same circuit as The Kids, the Rock Angels were also from Florida. He came in to make up for the shortcomings left by the departure of the guitar player. They performed quite well with each other and hoped for a great career in the music industry since glam rock was the rage at the time.

For various reasons, Depp went on to star in two additional films throughout this time period, both of which were box office duds. Rob Marrow played Johnny's closest buddy in the first film, Private Resort. It was loaded up with the sort of rough parody and sexual hints that were extremely popular at that point. Despite the fact that the film was a flop when it was released, Johnny Depp's supporters love to bring it up as a fun fact. This time around, Johnny was cast in a television movie called Slow Burn. In this role, Johnny portrayed a millionaire's kid who was being sought out by his father in a Hitchcock-style mystery. Despite the fact that this picture has only been watched by a small number of people, several commentators have praised the young Depp's performance. While some speculate that Johnny intentionally omits these two films from his resume, he has stated that he "made some shitty movies when he first started out, but that he's not uncomfortable with them, especially as he didn't think that he was going to be an actor. He was just trying to make some money. He was still a musician. Even if his genuine goals had not yet been realized, he was still working on financing them.

After this, Jacobs contacted and urged him to audition for a role in Oliver Stone's war film Platoon. Depp has been looking for a position like this for quite a while. He appreciated the composition and expected a section in it. After meeting with Stone, the director was so impressed by Johnny that he immediately contacted Jacobs and gave him the role. So, Johnny was able to go to the Philippine Islands to begin "boot camp" training for the movie. Sherilyn's name was scrawled over his helmet as a reminder of how much he missed her. They had to undergo grueling training in over 100-degree heat for thirteen days with the rest of the cast in the midst of a jungle. During the early stages of development, there were days when nothing seemed to be happening, but that was exactly how it was anticipated to operate in the end. During these unexpected twists and turns, it's probably nice to take comfort in the fact that everything will work out in the end, so you can move forward. In addition to the usual set and boot camp issues, Johnny's first feature film experience was marked by a number of unusual occurrences. As soon as the shooting was over, Johnny returned to the United States. Platoon was the highest-grossing picture of the year, with an estimated $8.1 million in ticket sales. After seeing Johnny's position reduced by more than half and severely harmed, Stone felt very sorry for him.

Fenn's one-night encounters with Johnny led to an on-again, off-again turbulent affair for the two of them. When it came to relationships, he kept true to his origins and strong upbringing, even if he was labeled as a wild youngster. In his mind, the honesty and transparency that may have caused the difficulties were never issues. According to his own admission, "I guess I am a blend of a realist and a romantic. I am quite attentive to the sentiments of others. As much as I value the stability and security that comes with a committed relationship, I'm also open to the possibility of divorce. It's possible to remain married for 50 or 75 years in a culture where people divorce every five minutes. In sum, he was doing the right thing by admitting that he was wrong when his friend said his latest project turned out poorly. The choice to go in a different direction worked well for their friendship. On the advice of Nicholas Cage, Johnny started attending the Loft Studio about this time. Johnny was certain that if he ever managed to get a significant job, he would devote time to honing his acting skills. Johnny was only there for a short time when Jacobs phoned again and offered him a television deal that would change everything.

Chapter Two

Personal Life

At this point in his life, Danny, Johnny's brother, lent him a print of Jack Kerouac's "On the Road." He said that reading this book would transform his whole outlook on life, including how he saw himself and what he aspired to achieve in the future. Even though he had never been a big fan of reading, he still had little passion for learning in class. While reading, Johnny stated he felt as if the book was speaking directly to him, encouraging him to absorb the material and apply it to his own life. He began to envision a higher presence, one that he had never seen or experienced before in his life. The entire day, it was obvious to him that he wanted something somewhat strange. It occurred to him that there was a totally separate world out there. He turned out to be increasingly more mindful of what was happening. Investigate crafted by Gregory Corso and Allen Ginsberg. He was an insatiable buyer of artistic expression. As Johnny put it, the educators and motivation he was looking for were "all over the place." In the end, Johnny did the unfathomable and left school, seeing more noteworthy assurance in a different kind of life. It was revealed at one of their meetings that he had already planned out his next move. My instructor took one glance at me and said, "I just don't really accept that secondary school is for you." The service he performed for me was enormous.

Following his lifelong ambition of becoming a rock star was at the heart of Johnny's brilliant scheme. After moving out of his mother's home, Johnny found a job at a petrol station in town. To help him cope, he formed a rock band called The Kids and purchased a 1956 cream Fender Telecaster as a memento. Inspired by Keith Richards and other well-dressed guitarists, he continued to follow in their footsteps. Bandmates' elder sister, Lori Allison, was dating him at the time. Johnny and Lori's relationship became stronger as the band's career progressed. Fans of The Kids were growing and they began opening for artists like the B-52s, The Pretenders, and Talking Heads. When Iggy Pop invited them to open for him in 1981, it was a huge success for them. Despite the fact that Iggy was a major influence on Johnny's music, an opportunity like this didn't appear to sink in. While drinking that night, Johnny began to behave strangely around Iggy, yelling comments like, "You think you're better than me?" A frustrated Iggy slammed the door on Johnny's head, calling him "a little turd." Johnny proposed to Lori because he still felt the grief of his parents' divorce and an empty heart, and she accepted immediately. Although Johnny was well aware of his advanced age at the time, when asked why he believed marriage would give him "strength," he admitted. In light of their triumph, the groups decided to take the next step. They decided to follow Don Ray's advice and go to California in quest of a record deal. From Florida to California, they gathered up their savings and set out. While waiting for their lucky break in California, Six Gun Method changed their name back to Six Gun Method. Johnny was well aware of the wide range of jobs he might take on to make ends meet. He was a repairman, a laborer, and a screen printer, notwithstanding other random temp jobs.

Johnny and Lori got hitched on December 20th, 1983. After he married Lori, Johnny began with an ordinary permit to sell pens as a sales rep. In fact, "Indeed, it resembled another part for each call," he says, snickering and downplaying what is happening. The only way to avoid becoming numb and lifeless was to switch things up. When Lori and Johnny realized their marriage was failing, they called it quits. Johnny has never made a public remark about the breakup and has kept that area of his personal life secret. Johnny's destiny was altered permanently because of Lori's exposure to him, even if they were on their way to splitting up.

Chapter Three

Becoming a Teen Idol

Johnny pondered on the opportunity to appear on the television program "21 Jump Street." He was adamant about not having a deal that might tie him down for an indeterminable period of time. But he also thought that, emerging from a highly acclaimed picture like Platoon, risking on a fresh, unproven television program was not something he was ready to do. Once questioned about the first phone call, Johnny said, "It was a good one." "It was with much reluctance that he agreed to go on the program when they phoned and requested it. So they had someone else sign his long-term deal since he refused to sign some massive document. It took approximately a month before they phoned me again to ask if he would kindly dismiss him. According to his representatives, TV programs typically have a thirteen-episode run. In the end, he consented to the arrangement. This decision was based partially on the guarantee of monetary dependability and a constant flow of profit. The primary task for the makers was to finish the pilot episode. Investigator Tom Hanson (Johnny's personality) was a cop who appeared to be excessively youthful for his situation. Hanson had a point to make to his bosses, who peered down on him. An opportunity to work as an undercover agent to safeguard and arrest high school students is presented to him. The massive anti-drug efforts of the mid-1980s coincided with the meteoric rise of 21 Jump Street. Because he couldn't commit to both the band and the TV program, Johnny had to give up his position with the Rock City Angels. While it may have appeared like Johnny missed out at the moment, Greffen Records signed the band to a 6.2 million dollar deal, and a few months later, the label left them, and Johnny was still on the program. A Vancouver, Canada-based Production Company was hired to film the show, and Johnny moved there. After shooting there for a few months, Johnny relocated his maternal grandparents to live with him. For the sake of her acting and film career, Sherilyn Fenn resisted the idea of joining him in relocating to New York with him. As a result of Johnny and Fenn's frequent trips back and forth, and professional obligations, Fenn debuted in an early scene on Jump Street.

It wasn't long until Johnny had a hard time playing Tom Hanson. According to Johnny, this is the case. In my opinion, there is no need for undercover officers to be stationed at high schools. Toward the day's end, it's just a question of reconfirmation. As per him, "the most compelling thing I escaped from our discussion was that we were especially in total agreement." This is what happened: Johnny was paid $45,000 for each show, which is a lot. Although the money was great, he felt isolated, and having his mom there was a big help for him. The program was a huge hit as soon as the first episode aired. The program had a large cast, but something about Johnny pushed him to the forefront of attention above all of the others. Johnny had no idea what to expect in this circumstance. The producers, on the other hand, saw it as a fantastic opportunity and jumped at the chance to get Johnny into every adolescent magazine they could. He was completely unprepared to deal with yet another situation like this. Johnny couldn't believe the devoted admirers' swooning over him, since he thought he was just an average person. Some of the tasks he had to do in his new role included fifteen-hour days of script memorizing, as well as fittings and picture shootings with a pistol. This was the time in his life when he understood that a large chunk of his laborious efforts had finally paid off, according to his evaluation of the circumstance. Many remarks have been made by Johnny regarding this point in his life, but "But these are things that are beyond his control" remains relevant today. Although it's a wonderful feeling to be praised, he was apprehensive about it. Becoming the center of attraction has never been his favorite thing to do. Isn't that how it goes sometimes? "

When he asked Fenn to marry him, his life took another turn for the better. As a result, the girls perceived Johnny as a lovely man, and his popularity continued to climb, despite the fact that this may have injured him. It wasn't long before the fan letters started pouring in from all around the world. For more than a year, Fan Handle declared that Johnny was the most popular actor in the world and got more than 10,000 pieces of mail a month. "Some of the letters in the alphabet are downright bizarre. They annoy him as well, saying if he doesn't write, will they kill themselves or seek advice? So who can he trust to provide counsel when he's not all that stable? "After a while, Johnny became exceedingly upset because he realized that there was a much wider difference between his everyday reality and the camera's perspective than he had expected.

Chapter Four

An Early Film Career

During filming and in everyday life, Johnny had begun to vent his frustrations. As he has said, it just wasn't rebelling, it was simply feeling awkward in his own body. Be that as it may, to other people who were curious about him, he was seen as a maverick. At a certain point in a meeting with (Rolling Stone 2008), he remarked that he was an imbecile. His sentiment with Fenn was slowing down now, and he was spotted all over town with a couple of different VIPs, most notably Jennifer Gray (from Dirty Dancing). On the arrangement of 21 Jump Street, he is said to have lit his underwear ablaze and made up the story as he came. He would think of his own ludicrous screenplay thoughts, accepting this was a method for defaming the contents he was discontent with. Scripts, according to Johnny, ought to be more "updated" and reflect what today's youth are going through in their existence. Even while some people may have thought these recommendations were out of left field, they were sincere efforts to bring Johnny's opinions on vital subjects to light. He was likewise disappointed with the way that the program continued to request that he chat on different themes, over which he accepted he had no power to address the crowd. "As a high school dropout, they wanted me to appear in these public service advertisements urging students to remain in school, even though everyone around me was aware of my situation. He said he couldn't stare those children in the eyes and scream "hypocrisy!"

Following years of being trapped in an impenetrable situation, he was finally ready to accept his next picture, "Cry Baby."

To his surprise, John Waters personally sent him a letter extending the invitation. When Johnny first saw the screenplay, he was ecstatic at the prospect of parodying his "teen idol image." For Johnny, this satire was precisely what he needed. At the same time, a creative endeavor that would enable him to extend his wings and burn off some steam at the same time. At the same time, Waters sought a young guy who could attract a more "cool" audience because he could stand back and laugh at himself. When he met Johnny, he found exactly the kind of job player he was looking for. Johnny was beautiful, eager to take on a new challenge, and willing to throw concealment at the person he was trying to get rid of. It was a walk in the park for Waters, who was anxious to get everything rolling. He was considerably more pleased when John requested that he give his own considerations and commitments to the screenplay during shooting. "John would really need to hear my considerations, but he could proceed to draw with me while I disliked a section of the image," he said. He's the only filmmaker I've worked with who's willing to go that far. "In spite of the fact that Johnny did not sing in the film's musical parts, he was heavily engaged in the selection of antique guitars and amplifiers for use in the film. Johnny could not only feign to play the guitar, but he could also demonstrate his abilities in person. This was one more justification for why he chose to assume this liability. Johnny's fellow actors in the film quickly realized that Johnny was a delight on set, and he struck up friendships with many of them, which he maintained for years to come. They found him to be diligent, devoted, and open to new experiences and learning. There are few young stars like Johnny Depp, said Waters, "who embrace criticism and recommendations with open arms." In different nations, Cry Baby turned out to be significantly more well-known than in the United States. To some extent, this happened on the grounds that the class lost its allure to the energetic American public. It had become old-fashioned to them, as it was related to the obsolete idea of 1950s rock and roll, exemplified by Elvis Presley. Even though he still had to return to season 21 for one more season, Cry Baby allowed him to start losing his skin.

The Great Balls of Fire premiered around this time, and Johnny met Winona Ryder there (1989). Their story goes that they crossed in the foyer and fell in love at first sight. It was "a classic gaze, such as in West Side Story, when all of it else got blurry," Johnny is reported as saying. After a couple of months, a companion of theirs recommended them to one another. After meeting Winona and falling in love, it was like nothing he had ever experienced before. The two became "Hollywood's newest romance" after discovering they had a lot in common. Of course, the media and the newspapers covered their romance, and it's still spoken about today. Although it has been several decades since this period in Johnny's life, it still serves as a period in his self-reputation. The movie Edward Scissor Hands was the next project on Johnny's radar. His request for Winona to act beside him in the film had been met with a yes from her. For various reasons, she was unable to fulfill her promise to some other picture, so she welcomed the film offer. Tim Burton, an up-and-coming filmmaker, directed the picture. This notion was born out of Tim's own difficulty expressing himself as a youngster. His concerns about America's reluctance to embrace diversity itself were so strong that he felt he needed to write a screenplay for Edward to help communicate them. Edward, the protagonist, had a new hairdo and a pallid complexion. Without his hands, he could not interact with anything around him or with himself. "As soon as he began reading, he couldn't put the book down," Johnny has said of the character he was required to play. For all intents and purposes, could the producer ever have faith in or knowledge of him as Edward? The meeting was held immediately because Johnny viewed this as an opportunity. The two of them had no clue how this fortuitous meeting would alter the course of their lives. The Bel Age

Hotel's coffee cafe in Los Angeles is where they first met. In front of them was a pair of people who, despite their ability to think outside the box, stumbled and stammered while attempting to communicate. You can tell just by conversing with them that they have a common mindset and perspective, yet there's also an uneasy sensation when it comes to sharing their views and opinions with one another. Johnny and Tim reminisced about their initial encounter a number of times. According to Johnny, "We closed the encounter with a handshake and a "glad to meet you" after bumbling our way through each other's incomplete statements, but yet still understanding one another." "Johnny is very much renowned as a teen idol, and he's viewed as tough and distant," Tim has remarked of his first encounter with Johnny. When it comes to his personality, he's a joy to be around. This individual appears to be standard, basically to me, but in all actuality, he is the specific inverse of what I thought he was. A subject close to his heart, identity and impression, or how someone is regarded to be something other than what they really are, was Edward's. "He was pleased to see Winona in the other main part, since he had previously worked with her on Beetlejuice. This was a very challenging moment for Johnny, and he relied heavily on the advice and guidance of the other more experienced performers on the set. Moreover, he described Edward as possessing "the purity of a new-born or the spontaneous affection of a dog" because of his uniqueness. As a young actor, Johnny felt like he had a male role model in Vincent Price, whom he bonded with throughout the production and kept in touch with after the film's release. It was challenging for Johnny at first, but he quickly got used to it and no longer had any problems moving about or living in the outfit. Several incidents with the blades occurred during the filming of the show, including one when Johnny accidentally pierced Anthony Michael Hall's character on the arm during a confrontation with Edward. Anthony reassured Johnny, "It's OK, dude," as he repeatedly apologized to him. Johnny was greatly inspired by his time on Edward Scissor Hands. As a "movie-creating monster," he made new pals and relied on their guidance as he began his career in filmmaking. As an actor, being complacent and stuck in your ways can be a real problem! Take Johnny's character, for example: he didn't want to slip into a rut, and Depp was getting tired of feeling like he was repeating himself. One of the reasons why he had stopped calling his friend so often lately was that he felt like they never had anything new to talk about. In comparison, one might say that happiness is preventing growth. Perhaps it was because he was so unhappy earlier in life that Johnny gravitated towards work that interested him as a means of expressing himself.

Chapter Five

Musical Career

"I never thought of acting, but you had to pay rent, bills... You had to look for alternatives. "

When Johnny Depp's relatives played music, he grew fascinated with it. A 12-year-old youngster has trained himself to play the acoustic guitar by hearing music and watching YouTube tutorials. While forming his own band in commemoration of his then-girlfriend Meredith, he played in a number of garage bands. Aside from the Belgian band, The Kids, he also established Flame, which he performed with in the 1980s. According to the musician, he was forced to take a break from music to focus solely on acting due to financial issues.

For the film "Chocolate" (2000), he performed electric guitar, and for the album "Érase Una Vez en México," he contributed vocals and guitar (2003). They worked on Shane MacGowan's first solo album since they were acquainted with the Pogues' Shane MacGowan. He belonged to the "P" gang as well. He also appeared in videos for Tom Petty & the Heartbreakers' "Into the Great Wide Open" and Radiohead's "Creep," among others. Aside from "You're So Vain" and "Queenie Eye," Marilyn Manson and Paul McCartney collaborated on "You're So Vain."

Another hard rock supergroup with Alice Cooper and Joe Perry, called "Hollywood Vampires," was founded by him as a guitarist. On September 11 of that year, they released their debut album, which had two songs written by Johnny Depp. At the Roxy Theater in Los Angeles and at the Rock in Rio music event in Brazil, he played with the band twice in September.

Chapter six

The Turbulent Times

Following the completion of "What's Eating Gilbert Grape," Johnny's private life took a dramatic turn for the worse. In 1989, he met actress Winona Ryder, with whom he began dating in 1990, and had her name tattooed on his arm. Johnny and Winona had a tumultuous marriage that was exacerbated by the media's obsession with them. There could have been no further reunions in 1993. It was a "pleasing partition," as per Johnny, yet the press guaranteed "unavoidable character issues." Therefore, Johnny had the option of requiring his own life to be postponed for some time. "Ed Wood," a black-and-white biography of the failed filmmaker, was their second collaboration with Tim Burton.

In Johnny's words, he said he was committed within five minutes of hearing about this. This part provided a chance for Johnny to "stretch out and have some fun" since he was miserable about practically everything in his life, including films and filmmaking, at the time. An accurate depiction of an incorrect guy was how one reviewer praised the film, despite a poor box office performance (possibly owing to its restricted distribution).

Suffering and depression

After purchasing The Viper Club in Los Angeles with two key stakeholders in August 1993, it became the hottest location on the Sunset Strip almost overnight. When Johnny Depp created his band P, he took advantage of the club's popularity by performing live gigs for the band's fans. River Phoenix, a teen idol and highly renowned actor, died of a drug overdose outside the club on October 31st of that year. In the late hours of the night, Phoenix surrendered to her injuries and passed away.

Also, Depp toyed with narcotics and became depressed. While Kate Moss was seeing him at this time, he began a very public connection. In 1994, Depp notoriously damaged a New York hotel room following one of the couple's frequent disagreements with a scuffle between the two of them.

As a result of his crazy antics, Johnny Depp's professional career seemed to remain unaffected. A documentary about legendary B-movie filmmaker Ed Wood co-starred him and Burton again in 1994. In addition to receiving critical praise, Depp was nominated for a second Golden Globe. Two more significant films from the late 1990s that featured Depp as an undercover cop are Donnie Brasco (1997) and Don Juan DeMarco (1995), in which

Depp portrays a guy who thinks he is Don Juan.

In addition to playing Hunter S. Thompson's alter persona, Depp divorced from long-term lover Moss and starred in Terry Gilliam's version of Fear and Loathing in Las Vegas. The bond between Depp and Thompson developed throughout the production and continued after Thompson's death in 2005, with Depp financing the author's burial.

In spite of this, Johnny shut down the club the next year on the commemoration of River's passing. Notwithstanding this, Johnny's own life was self-destructing at a disturbing rate, and he purportedly said that it appeared like, all in all, nothing remained in his life to live for. When Johnny was arrested in New York in 1994 for vandalizing a hotel suite, all he could explain was that the room had been destroyed by an armadillo. Refusing to leave, he insisted on paying for the accommodation when the security personnel urged him to. Reaching out to the police was his only option because there was no other way he could defend himself. He regretted that it had come to this, especially since it meant he'd have to be in a police uniform while being taken away. It's no surprise that the media didn't let this episode go unreported, instead using it to play into Johnny's reputation as a "Hollywood bad-boy". It was widely reported that Johnny was in handcuffs, and massively inaccurate versions of the tale were circulating. For a very long time, Depp got into the limelight, but he wasn't really after the attention any longer. Destroying hotel property was known as "doing the Johnny Depp".

While the rumors swirled around Johnny, he opted to ignore them and focus on his next movie, "Nick of Time," in which he starred as Gene Watson, a mild-mannered gunman who kills a governor in order to free his kidnapped daughter. Even though it made more money than it cost to make, this forgettable thriller only brought in roughly $8 million. A particular waif-like model, however, would soon bring Depp back to prominence in the media spotlight.

After completing Ed Wood in 1994, Johnny met Kate. "At the time, both of us were flourishing on smokes and barely sleeping," Johnny Depp is believed to have stated. As he was "Hollywood's Current It-Boy" and she was a high-profile model, their relationship was well publicized. On several occasions, Johnny came to Kate's defense against the "anorexic" moniker, claiming that she "ate as well as any guy I know." While looking up media outlets, Johnny realized that some things he said during the filming phase of Project Mayhem would be twisted around as people made inferences that could paint a wrong

picture of him to the public.

Chapter Seven

Upheaving Times

Like his connection with Winona, Johnny and Kate's romance was a focus of the media, since Kate was also a relatively introverted person. When Johnny wasn't protecting each other's professions and reputations, he starred in Dead Man. When a bookkeeper lost both of his folks and met Nobody in this gun-slinging, acid-western, Dead Man was a black-and-white, grainy, independent picture that received decent reviews. On the other hand, Johnny, on the other hand, went on to play the character of the world's greatest lover, Don Juan DeMarco, after leaving this position.

It's no surprise that "Don Juan" was a box office smash, with an estimated $41 million worldwide. In "Johnny," he portrays an attempted suicide who recounts how his background caused him to believe he was Don Juan DeMarco, the world's best lover. Despite the fact that Johnny's movie was very sentimental, the media was always hounding him about his personal love life, leading to several reports of breakups that he rejected. However, Johnny's craziest moment was when he was with Kate.

"The Brave" was Johnny's directorial debut after his cameo role in Cannes Man was completed. A short film about a guy who signs up for a snuff film in order to get money for his family (a torture and death film). Johnny's next project after that was Donnie Brasco, a crime-drama-thriller starring Al Pacino, and he got to work on it right away. As part of a new project, Johnny met Hunter S. Thompson, who would go on to become a close friend and mentor until his tragic death in 2005. As Johnny portrayed Raoul Duke in Hunter's novel, Fear and Loathing in Las Vegas, the two became fast friends.

Despite the fact that they were extremely content with one another, the two of them needed to encounter something else and afterward headed out in different ways tactfully. The press was in a tizzy, but they couldn't be sure if Johnny and Kate had broken up or not since they lived such private lives. "Honk if you're engaged to Johnny Depp!" was placed on car stickers, alluding to his "dog" conduct. After Johnny stated that he wasn't "good enough" for her, he went on to say that he lived a life that consisted of him "going home, sobbing, not sleeping, eating, and drinking beer."

Even though he had just broken up with Kate, Johnny noticed a return. Vanessa Paradis was the French singer and supermodel who would become the man's companion for the next 13 years after he changed again. Following his encounter with Vanessa, Johnny's "wild kid" persona seemed to have faded. One of his contentious portions in 1999 sparked a confrontation between him and the photographers involved.

Aside from that event, Johnny's career continued as usual, with roles in films such as The Ninth Gate, a horror film about a book that has the power to call the devil, a cameo in L.A. Without a Map, and Tim Burton's Sleepy Hollow, a cinematic adaptation of the long-told, spooky fairy tale. When it came to being a father that was Johnny's first step. To become a father, he would need to take many more

steps after this one.

Chapter Eight

Relationship Crises and Legal Tussle

Rumors started to spread in 2012 that Johnny and Paradis had officially separated. He first rejected the reports, but in June, a spokesman for the actor confirmed the couple's split. When queried by Entertainment Tonight, Depp's spokesperson stated the couple "has peacefully split" and urged that the public "respect their privacy" and that of the actor's children. Before their breakup, Depp and Paradis had been together for almost 14 years.

On the set of a film, Depp met a new lover while he was still dating Paradis. While shooting The Rum Diary, he met Amber Heard, his co-star. They first appeared together in public in 2012, shortly after Johnny's breakup with Paradis. On Christmas Eve 2013, the pair got engaged and married in February of the following year.

When Heard filed for divorce in May 2016, she also sought a court injunction against Johnny, claiming he had been emotionally and physically manhandling her throughout their marriage. The divorce was completed in January 2017 after a settlement was agreed in August. The actor launched a $50 million defamation claim against his ex-wife after she wrote an op-ed in December 2018 detailing her past with domestic abuse.

To get back at the people who squandered Depp's riches over the past few years, Johnny launched a $25 million lawsuit in October 2017 against his previous business managers. When two former personal security guards sued Depp in April of that year, he was on the receiving end of a lawsuit for unpaid salaries and unsafe working conditions.

Depp said that he was acting in self-defense because Brooks's "illegitimate and unjust actions" had made him "fear for his life."

Political views

For Depp, "America is foolish, is like a silly dog with large teeth—that may bite and injure you, aggressive," he said in 2003 to the German magazine Stern. Stern and CNN both stuck by their stories, despite Stern's claims that the magazine misreported and misrepresented his comments. According to CNN, Trump made the comment that he would want his children to think of the United States as "a toy, a shattered toy". "Experiment with it for a while, see whether you like it, and then leave." According to Depp, later media portrayals of him as a "European wannabe" were inaccurate, and he has said that when living in France with Paradis, he preferred the obscurity and simplicity of the country. To avoid paying taxes twice, Depp moved back to the United States in 2011 when France asked him to apply for permanent residency.

Also, to help free Ukrainian cinematographer Oleg Sentsov, Depp teamed up with the Detained for Art campaign, which he engaged in November 2016. When Depp was questioned during the 2017 Glastonbury Festival, "The last time an actor murdered a President?" A clarification: in response to Trump's criticism, a clarification: saying he is not a professional actor. He makes a livelihood by telling lies. There is a possibility that it's been a while, and it may be time. "He's not claiming anything. The assassination of Abraham Lincoln by actor John Wilkes Booth was cited as the inspiration for the remark. For security purposes, they could not disclose directly or in broad terms how they fulfill their protection obligations, "Secret Service spokesman Shawn Holtzclaw told CNN. "We are aware of Depp's statement." Later, Depp issued an apology, claiming the phrase did not come out as intended and that he meant no animosity.

Alcohol and drug use.

For much of his life, Johnny Depp has fought with drinking and drug abuse.

Johnny claims to have started doing drugs at the age of eleven after taking his mom's "nociceptive pills," started blunt at 12, and had tried "every sort of substance there was" by the time he was 14. While shooting What's Eating Gilbert Grape, Johnny Depp admitted to drinking excessively (1993). In an interview broadcast in 2008, actor Johnny Depp said that he had been infested by liquor for years. He said that he examined wine and spirits completely, and they surely examined him too, though, "Depp stated, but they figured out that they got together brilliantly, but maybe too well, when asked why he had quit drinking in 2013. Depp stated he "certainly wasn't going to depend on the booze to smooth things or cushion the blow or cushion the situation because it might have been catastrophic" after his split from longtime lover Vanessa Paradis.

Amber Heard claims that during their marriage, Depp "plummeted into the depths of psychosis and violence after feasting on drugs and booze" throughout their marriage. Furthermore, Depp called the claim made by his former business managers that he spent $30,000 a month on wine "disgusting," since he had spent "much more" than this amount. Actor Johnny Depp acknowledged at his libel trial in 2020 that he was addicted to

Roxicodone and drank heavily throughout his relationship with Amber Heard.

Chapter Nine

Johnny Depp v. Ex-Wife Amber Heard:
Defamation Trial in 2022

They're fighting in a suburban courthouse in Washington, D.C., after divorcing in 2011. This is a libel case. Following the publication of her essay in the Washington Post supporting the Violence against Women Act, Depp's ex-wife, Heard, is suing him for $100 million for defamation and Depp is suing an counter lawsuit of $50m

It was common for Heard to be harassed and physically molested by the time she was in college. "But she kept her mouth shut because she didn't believe that submitting a complaint would result in fairness. In addition, she said she didn't think of herself as a victim. Now that she's an advocate for domestic violence victims, she's been hit with the full weight of our society's fury for women who speak up. "

Johnny Depp made by Heard during their divorce in 2016. The couple's year-long relationship came to an end without the need for a courtroom battle. In the midst of the intense media attention, Depp and Heard released a joint statement that said, in part, "To date, neither side has made any false charges with the intention of gaining an advantage." I never intended to damage someone physically or emotionally. Amber hopes for the best for Johnny's future endeavors. "

The 58-year-old actor now accuses the 35-year-old actress of defaming him in her article since, according to his attorneys, it references other charges she's made against him. Jurors and alternates (who were screened to see whether they were familiar with the actors' previous film roles) started deliberations in the libel trial in Fairfax, Virginia, on Monday. Because of the proximity of The Washington Post's computer servers, the venue was chosen. Additionally, the courtroom's isolation from the paparazzi culture of Los Angeles and New York is undoubtedly a contributing factor.

Celebs like Paul Bettany, James Franco, and Tesla CEO Elon Musk are expected to appear in court, and the paparazzi may be unable to stop them.

There's a good chance this test may go on for a month or more.

Made in the USA
Monee, IL
14 May 2022

96395944R00057